AN
EXALTATION
of
BUSINESS
AND
FINANCE

To _____

From _____

ALSO BY JAMES LIPTON

An Exaltation of Larks
Mirrors
An Exaltation of Larks, The Ultimate Edition

AN EXALTATION *of* BUSINESS AND FINANCE

James Lipton
Author of *AN EXALTATION OF LARKS*

DESIGNED BY KEDAKAI LIPTON

Villard Books, New York 1993

We wish to extend thanks to *Harper's Weekly,*
Ladies' Home Journal, The New York Public Library
(Print Division; General Research Division; Astor,
Lenox and Tilden Foundations' Keppler Collection),
the British Library, British Library Reproductions
for "Chancery Lane Safe Deposit," the collections
of the Library of Congress.

Grateful acknowledgment is made to Penguin Books USA Inc. for
permission to reprint 24 terms from *An Exaltation of Larks* by James Lipton.
Copyright © 1968, 1977, 1991 by James Lipton. Reprinted by permission of
Viking Penguin, a division of Penguin Books USA Inc.

Library of Congress Cataloging-in-Publication Data
Lipton, James.
An exaltation of business and finance/James Lipton; designed by
Kedakai Lipton.—1st ed.
p. cm.
ISBN 0-679-41869-5
1. Business—Humor.   2. Finance—Humor.   3. American wit and
humor.   I. Title.
PN6231.B85L52   1993
818'.5402—dc20   93-18287

Book and Illustration Design by Kedakai Lipton

Manufactured in the United States of America on acid-free paper
9 8 7 6 5 4 3 2
First Edition

PRELUDE

The English language's unique habit of assigning to groups of animals an imaginative, often witty, sometimes poetic or sardonic, but always surprising and illuminating term began in 1323 when King Edward II's huntsman, Master William Twici, undertook to codify the language of a gentleman's only peacetime occupation: hunting. Master Twici's book, written in Norman French, was called *Le Art de Venery*, the word *venery* deriving from the same Latin sources as Venus and referring in this case to the hunter's passionate pursuit of his quarry. Six hundred forty-five years later, there was, oddly, still no proper collective for these fascinating collectives, so, inspired by Master Twici, I selected *terms of venery* to describe the subject of my book *An Exaltation of Larks*.

An exaltation of larks is, of course, a term of venery, which is to say it is, in my opinion, the proper term for a group of larks—as opposed, say, to a *school* or *pride* of larks. If *school* and *pride* of larks sound peculiar, it's because, since the fourteenth century, the English language has retained its curious venereal habit, and most of us say a *school of fish* or *pride of lions* (or *host of angels*) without realizing we are using terms of venery invented and codified more than six hundred years ago.

Today we'd provoke snickers if we said *a herd of fish* or *a school of elephants,* but in the fifteenth century such a gaffe would have been shocking, and so would anything but *an exaltation of larks, a sloth of bears, a leap of leopards,* or *a murder of crows.* A young gentleman of that period had to learn by rote *all* the terms of venery, and to assist him numerous manuscripts and books were written on the subject, each one including what the scribe or author considered to be a definitive list.

1486 was a venereal watershed, for in that year, only a decade after William Caxton introduced printing to England, the "schoolmaster printer" published *The Book of St. Albans* by Dame Juliana Barnes, with its historic list of 164 terms.

Five hundred years later, when I first sensed that *a pride of lions* and *a gaggle of geese* might be only the tip of a linguistic iceberg, I embarked on a journey that led me eventually to the Reading Room of the British Museum, where I held in my hands *The Book of St. Albans* and, turning Dame Juliana's pages at last, discovered that, side-by-side with *a skulk of foxes, a cowardice of curs* and *a shrewdness of apes,* were such antic inventions as *a bevy of ladies* (yes, Mr. Ziegfeld—in 1486), *a rascal of boys, a rage of maidens,* and *an incredulity of cuckolds* (yes, Mr. Hefner—in 1486).

In a language-besotted country that was about to give birth to an age of literary genius the likes of which the world had never seen, and will probably never see again, Dame Juliana and her contemporaries had turned "science" into art, solemn pedantry into airy fantasy, and the English language into a playground without fences.

In short, the venereal *game* had been born—which inspired and emboldened me, as I snatched *a charm of finches* and *an unkindness of ravens* back from the void into which they had vanished, to invent terms of venery for our own time: *a slouch of models, a wince of dentists, a charge of shoppers, a chisel of repairmen, a lot of realtors, a score of bachelors, a trance of lovers, a mass of Bostonians, a pocket of quarterbacks, a handful of gynecologists, a déjà gout of leftovers, an unction of undertakers* (in a larger group *an extreme unction of undertakers*) . . .

It was like eating peanuts: I couldn't stop. And neither, I'm happy to report, could the readers of *An Exaltation of Larks.* The book has remained in print from the day of its publication to the present, updated and expanded to the current 324-page *Ultimate Edition* by *a flood of venereal terms* from all over the world.

Now, here is still another batch, devoted this time to a single subject: *An Exaltation of Business and Finance.* Please join me in the game of venery, as it has been played by word lovers for nearly seven hundred years.

BIG BUSINESS

A carrot of bonuses
(*for the upper echelons:* carat)

A plutocracy of CEO's

A mishmash of co-CEO's

A draw of partners

An oversight of directors

A clamber of executives

A slumber of boardrooms

A burnout of VP's

A meddle of micromanagers

A crisis of middle managers

A snarl of negotiations

A roar of disagreements

A perseverance (*sometimes* persecution) of working women

A deluge of MBA's

A tangle of regulations
A plot of regulators

A ploy of deregulations
A clot of red tape

A pad of expense accounts

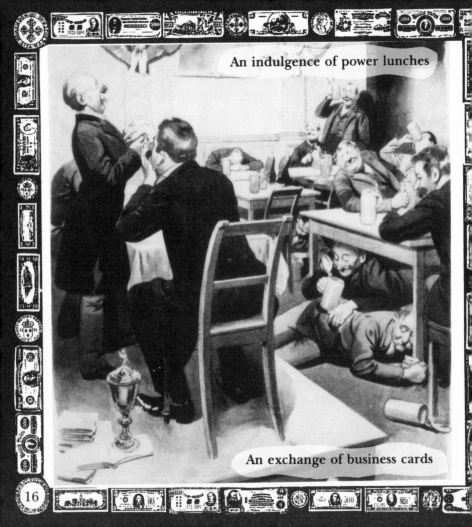

An indulgence of power lunches

An exchange of business cards

16

A bomb of firings

A balm of hirings

A fist of strikes
A freeze of lockouts
A safety net of unions *(from the workers' point of view)*
A featherbed of unions *(from the employers' point of view)*

A chore of business trips *(to Boise)*

A charm of business trips *(to Bali)*

18

A maze of trade fairs

A quarry of consumers

A burst of profits
A bust of losses

A firing squad of management consultants (*formerly,* time/motion analysts; *even more formerly,* efficiency experts)

SMALL BUSINESS

A worry of retailers
A sorry of wholesalers

A nurture of mom-and-pop stores
A nepotism of family businesses
An epidemic of franchises

21

An umbrella of sidewalk vendors

A leap of entrepreneurs

A charge of shoppers
A seizure of impulse buyers
A bait of bargains
A battle of sales
A line of salesmen
A ring of cashiers

A sprawl of malls

A riptide (*sometimes* ripoff) of markdowns

A riot of refunds

MERGER BUSINESS

A prowl of arbitrageurs

A clutch of corporate raiders

A counsel of investment bankers

A host of hostile takeovers

A bag of acquisitions

A big deal of venture capitalists

A milkin' of junk bonds

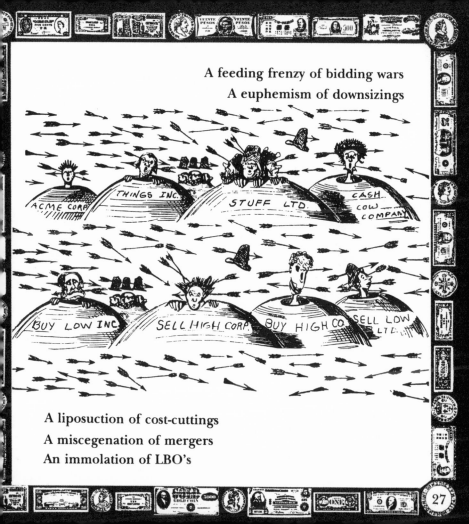

A feeding frenzy of bidding wars
A euphemism of downsizings

A liposuction of cost-cuttings
A miscegenation of mergers
An immolation of LBO's

A cache (*var.* cash) of crown jewel defenses
A vial (*var.* vile) of poison pills
A gobble of Pac Man strategies
A sting of killer bees
A spleen of greenmailers

A godsend of white knights   A rip of golden parachutes

EVERYBODY'S BUSINESS

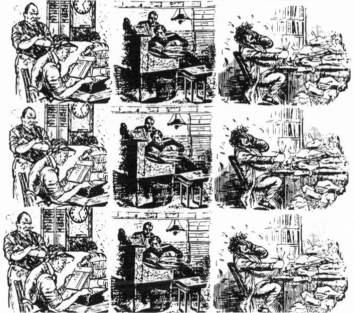

A column of accountants
A ho! ho! of loopholes
An oh! oh! of audits

A fantasy of exemptions
A siphon of taxes

A breakdown of plans (*as in, "The company has just issued its latest breakdown of plans."*)

A death row of deadlines

A crawl of messengers

A trial of lawsuits

An eternity of litigation

A jungle of want ads

A hemorrhage of pink slips

A flatline of layoffs

A watch of retirements

A cartel of cellular phones
A hail of beepers

A disinformation of answering services
An iron curtain of answering machines
A byte of computers

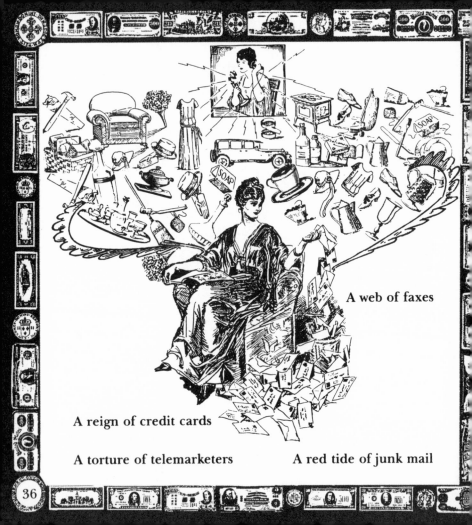

A web of faxes

A reign of credit cards

A torture of telemarketers

A red tide of junk mail

36

A deliverance of mailmen

A hammer of auctioneers

A caveat of auctions

A wheedle of insurance salesmen

A lot of realtors

An odd lot of used-car salesmen

NOBODY'S BUSINESS

A caper of capos

A magnum of hitmen
in pursuit of
A split of squealers

A patriarchy of godfathers

A con of consiglieri

A burrow of black marketeers

A shakedown of shylocks

MONEY BUSINESS

A riddle of economists

A mystery of recessions

An enigma of recoveries

A laff of supply-siders

A trickle of Reaganomics

A cavalry of Clintonians

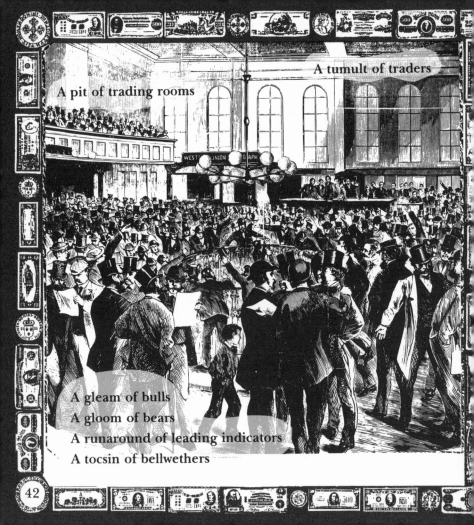

A pit of trading rooms

A tumult of traders

A gleam of bulls
A gloom of bears
A runaround of leading indicators
A tocsin of bellwethers

A roller coaster of stock markets
A split of stocks

A raze of dividends
A gambol of over-the-counter stocks
A commission of brokers
A margin of investors

A float of bonds   A tick of bond salesmen

A priority of bondholders

A tradeoff of capital markets

A controversy of capital gains

An evaporation of annuities

A cage of tellers

A supplication of borrowers

An interest of bankers
A Babel of currencies

A chapter of bankruptcies
A pigout of savings and loans

RAG MONEY
GAMES OF CHANCE
BETTING
GIFT ENTERPRISE
CAPITAL PRIZE $100000
INFLATION
GRAND PRIZE $100000
POLICY
PUBLIC OFFICE
JOCKEYING
RINGS
PUTS & CALLS
POOLS
THE CREDIT SYSTEM
SOMETHING FOR NOTHING
A LUCKY HIT
GAMBLING
FANCY STOCKS
RAILROAD BUBBLES
A BIG BONANZA
LOTTERY
SPECULATION
BOGUS SCHEME
GOLD MINE BUBBLE

A pop of balloon payments
A preserve of trust funds
A nest egg of IRA's
A sieve of pension plans

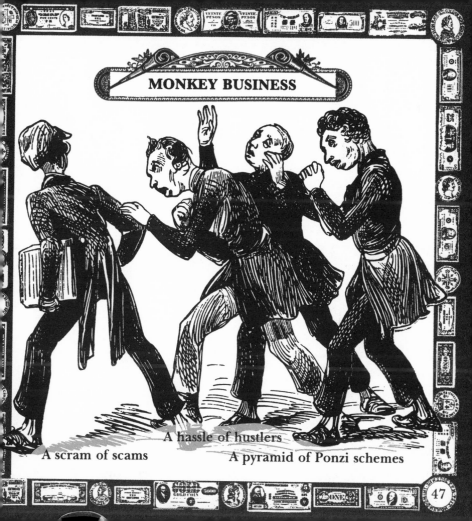

MONKEY BUSINESS

A hassle of hustlers

A scram of scams

A pyramid of Ponzi schemes

47

A humbug of con artists

A shilling of baits and switches

A slop of bucket shops

48

A flight of deadbeats

A pray of televangelists

A prey of their flocks

WHAT MAKES ALL THE WORLD DIVINE.

4 of £20,000!
ALL IN ONE DAY,
Next Tuesday
(13th APRIL.)

No Blanks, as every Number will be entitled to £5, Shares in proportion.

☞ Lotteries must entirely finish in a few Months.

A great variety of Numbers are selling by

HAZARD & CO
At their Old-established and Fortunate Offices,
Royal Exchange Gate; 26, Cornhill; & 324, Oxford Street, end of Regent Street;
Where, in the last Year's Lotteries ALONE, they sold
FIVE Prizes of £30,000 & £20,000!

Four £20,000
ALL IN ONE DAY,
Next Tuesday
(13th APRIL.)

No Blanks, as every Number will be entitled to £5, Shares in proportion.

☞ Lotteries must entirely finish in a few Months.

A great variety of Numbers are selling by

HAZARD & CO
At their Old-established and Fortunate Offices,
Royal Exchange Gate; 26, Cornhill; & 324, Oxford Street, end of Regent Street;
Where, in the last Year's Lotteries ALONE, they sold
FIVE Prizes of £30,000 & £20,000!

Modern Belles are very fine;
Modern Beaux are very funny;
But they both are thought divine,
When they've got a "Mint of Money."

How is that to be obtain'd?
Said a charming fair so pretty;
By the LOTTERY 'tis gain'd,
So purchase quickly, if you're witty.

ALL in One DAY!
FOUR of £20,000
Thirty other Capitals!
NO BLANKS!
ALL TO BE DRAWN.
ON TUESDAY,
19th APRIL.

A great Variety of Numbers on Sale by J. & J.

SIVEWRIGHT
CONTRACTORS,
37, Cornhill; 11, Holborn; and 38, Haymarket;
Who Sold in Shares in the last Contract

12,478 - - £30,000.

A mirage of lotteries
A lot—*not!*—of lottery winners

A pound of peddlers
A yen of panhandlers

MEDIA BUSINESS

A pitch of ad agencies
A bitch of clients

A spot of advertisers

A segment of media salesmen
A glut of commercials
A boast of promos

A spiel of announcers

A slide of ratings

An alarm of sponsors

A feed of satellites

A surcharge of pay-per-views

A panic of producers

A blight of billboards

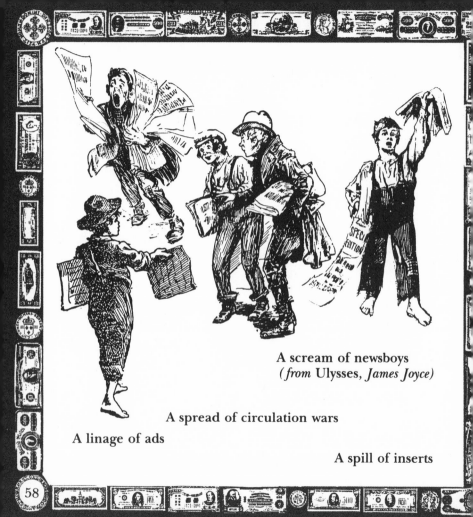

A scream of newsboys
(from Ulysses, *James Joyce)*

A spread of circulation wars

A linage of ads

A spill of inserts

A mixup of mailroom clerks

An anachronism of secretaries

An omnipotence of administrative assistants
(*formerly known as* secretaries)

An ogle of office boys

An avalanche of memos

A qwerty of typists

A Qwerty of beginning typists

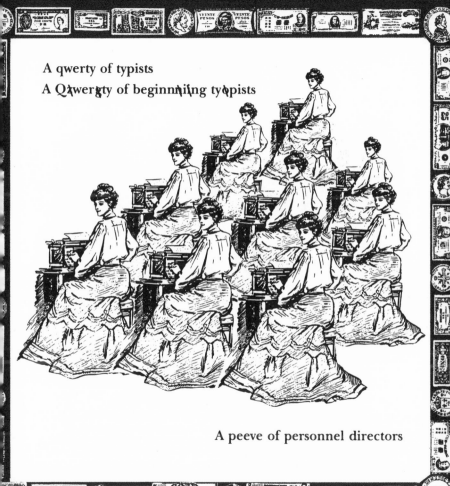

A peeve of personnel directors

A snooze of coffee breaks

A water hole of coolers

A cutup of office parties
A vale of farewell parties

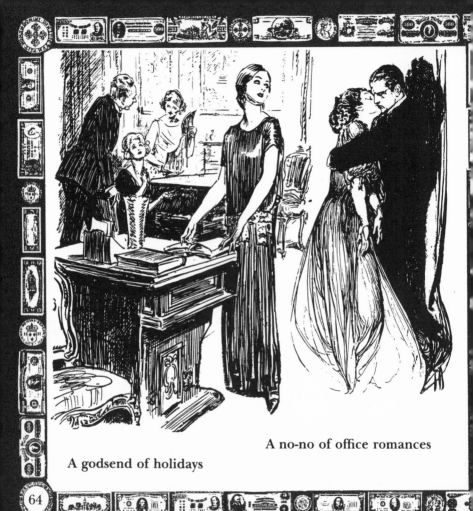

A no-no of office romances

A godsend of holidays